10 Minute

DECORATIVE CARDS

Annalees Lim

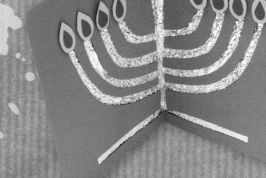

WAYLAND

First published in paperback in 2016 by Wayland

Copyright © Wayland, 2016

Dewey Number: 745.5'941-dc23
ISBN: 978 0 7502 9752 3
Ebook ISBN: 978 0 7502 9412 6
10 9 8 7 6 5 4 3 2

Printed in China

Wayland
An imprint of
Hachette Children's Group
Part of Hodder & Stoughton
Carmelite House
50 Victoria Embankment
London EC4Y 0DZ

An Hachette UK Company
www.hachette.co.uk
www.hachettechildrens.co.uk

Editor: Elizabeth Brent
Craft stylist: Annalees Lim
Designer: Elaine Wilkinson
Photographer: Simon Pask, N1 Studios

The website addresses (URLs) and QR codes included in this book were valid at the time of going to press. However, it is possible that contents or addresses may have changed since the publication of this book. No responsibility for any such changes can be accepted by either the author or the Publisher.

Picture acknowledgements:
All step-by-step craft photography: Simon Pask, N1 Studios;
images used throughout for creative graphics: Shutterstock

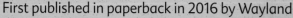

Contents

Decorative cards

Cards are a great way to let someone know you are thinking about them. Throughout the year, there are so many holidays and festivals that you will have no problem finding occasions to make cards for. The card ideas in this book only take about ten minutes to do, so if you are in a rush and need ideas fast, or just looking for a simple project you can make for all your family and friends, then this is the book for you!

Creating your own cards allows you to make each one unique, and extra special. Use materials that you find around you — recycling old cards is a great way to get creative and turn old artwork into new pictures. You can also cut them up into colourful mosaics, or even into shapes to use as templates. Old wrapping paper is useful to save, too, so start collecting any odd bits and pieces you come across, and keep them together for the next time you are getting crafty.

Personalise your cards by writing people's names on the front. Use colours or photographs that they like to make them extra special. You can also fill your cards full of fun surprises. If you are making a birthday card, you could enclose a balloon, or if you are celebrating a holiday, you could sprinkle some confetti inside, so that it falls out when the card is opened.

Crafting can be messy, especially if you are using glitter or glue, so make sure you cover all your work surfaces with old newspaper or a plastic tablecloth before you begin. Glues and paints will need to dry in a warm place before you start writing in your card. This will stop you from smudging any paint, and make sure that everything stays stuck in place. Always wash your hands after you have used glue to stop your works of art from being ruined by sticky fingers, and always ask an adult to help you with sharp scissors or compasses.

Whatever holiday you are celebrating, there is a card for the occasion! So, get out your craft materials, open your diary and start creating crafty cards for all your loved ones.

Valentine's Day card

Valentine's Day is celebrated every year on 14th February. It is traditional to send your loved ones handwritten notes, cards or gifts on this day to let them know how much you care about them. Try making this fun card, with a detachable heart-shaped badge!

Cut a large, a medium and a small heart shape out of the felt.

Sew the safety pin to the back of the largest felt heart.

Stick the felt hearts one on top of the other, using the fabric glue.

Fold the card in half and sew the buttons to each corner of the front, using the needle and thread.

5

Pin the heart to the front of the card. Make sure the glue is completely dry before writing your message inside.

It's not known exactly how the holiday began, but one story is that St. Valentine was a Roman priest, who was imprisoned for performing wedding ceremonies for soldiers who were forbidden to marry.

Easter card

You will need:
- Yellow A5 card
- Wrapping paper
- Scissors
- A glue stick
- A pencil and ruler
- Green and pink card
- Scrap card (for template)
- Ribbon

Easter is one of the oldest Christian festivals. It is known as a 'moveable feast' because the date changes every year. Eggs are associated with Easter because it always takes place in the spring, when baby chicks hatch. Make this card, with a 3D Easter egg, to wish someone a very Happy Easter!

Cover one side of the yellow card with a slightly smaller piece of wrapping paper, and glue it in place.

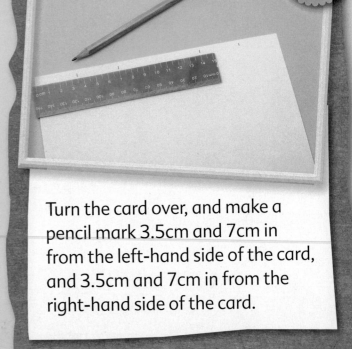

Turn the card over, and make a pencil mark 3.5cm and 7cm in from the left-hand side of the card, and 3.5cm and 7cm in from the right-hand side of the card.

3

Fold the sides of the card in towards the middle at the 7cm marks, and back out at the 3.5cm marks, to make two concertinas.

4

Use the scrap card make an egg template. Draw round this onto the front of the folded card, the green card and the pink card, then cut around all of the egg shapes.

5

Fold the green and pink eggs in half and stick one underneath each side of the yellow egg. Tie the ribbon in a bow around the card, sticking it down at the back.

In 2007, 10,000 children gathered at the world's largest Easter egg hunt in Florida, USA. More than half a million eggs were hidden for the children to find!

Watch this step-by-step video of the Easter card being made!

Mother's and Father's Day card

You will need:
- Blue card
- A glue stick
- Two wooden skewers
- Sticky tape
- White and patterned paper
- Scissors
- Thread

Mother's and Father's Days are celebrated in different months in different countries around the world. They are a time to celebrate our parents, often by giving cards and gifts. This card includes celebratory bunting!

1

Fold the blue card in half. Fold one edge back to the fold, then turn over and repeat on the other side.

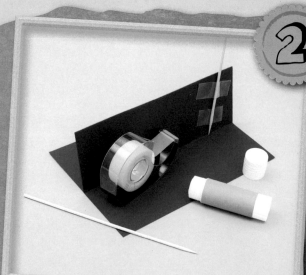

2

Glue the middle sections together to make a 'T' shape. Tape two skewers to one side of the upright piece of card.

3

Fold the patterned paper in half and cut out five triangles along the folded edge, to make five diamond shapes.

4

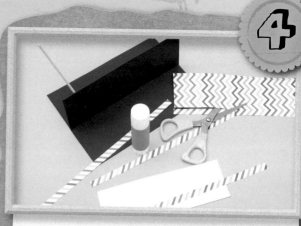

Cut out a rectangle of white paper and stick it to the front of the card to write your message on. Decorate the edge with some more patterned paper.

5

Tie or tape some thread between the sticks. Fold the diamonds over the thread to make bunting, sticking them in place with the glue stick.

Happy Mother's Day!

Father's Day only came into being after Mother's Day was officially declared a day to celebrate motherhood in America.

Birthday card

You will need:
- A piece of white card, 15×30cm
- coloured card
- Scissors
- Patterned paper
- A small candle
- Sticky pads
- Brown paper
- A paper cupcake case
- A glue stick
- White, yellow and orange paper

The anniversary of the day we were born is known as our birthday. People celebrate birthdays by giving gifts and sending cards. This birthday card comes with a birthday cake, complete with its very own candle!

1

Fold the white card in half and stick a slightly smaller square of coloured card to the front. Cut a rectangle of patterned paper, and stick it to the bottom of the card.

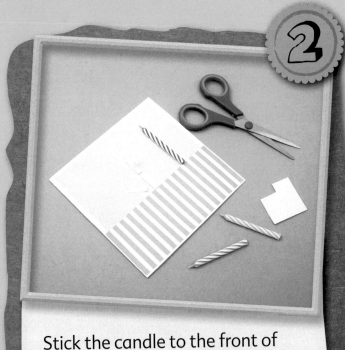

2

Stick the candle to the front of the card using the sticky pads.

3

Cut out a small semicircle of brown paper and stick this to the top of the rectangle, so it covers the bottom of the candle, using the sticky pads.

4

Cut a section from the cupcake case and stick this under the brown semicircle using a sticky pad.

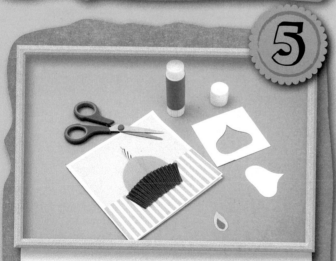

5

Make some cake frosting from white paper and a small flame from the yellow and orange paper and glue them both to the card.

The Happy Birthday song used to be called Good Morning to All. It was written by two American sisters in 1893.

Eid-Ul-Fitr card

You will need:

- A4 black and coloured card
- Scissors
- A pencil
- White card
- Tissue paper
- A glue stick
- Sticky tape

Eid is a Muslim festival marking the end of the fasting days of Ramadan. It is also called the Sweet Festival or Sugar Feast, because it is traditional to start the day with a small, sweet breakfast.

1

Fold a piece of black card into six equal sections and open it up into a concertina.

2

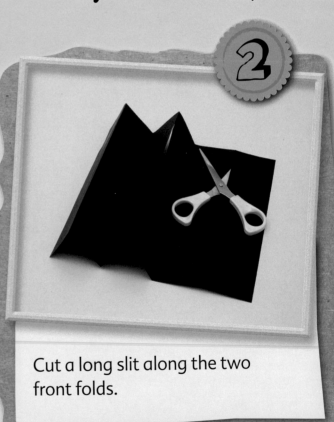

Cut a long slit along the two front folds.

3

Cut a piece of black card and a piece of coloured card the same widths as the slits. Draw building silhouettes on both, making sure the shapes on one are slightly higher than the shapes on the other, and cut them out.

4

Fold the white card in half and glue strips of tissue paper to the top half using the glue stick. Cut out a crescent moon from the coloured card, and stick it over the tissue paper.

5

Slot the building shapes into the two slits of the concertina, and stick this onto the bottom of the white card, using the sticky tape.

Eid-Ul-Fitr can last for one, two or three days, and begins when a new moon appears in the sky.

15

Christmas card

You will need:

- Double-sided tape
- Gold card
- Ribbons
- Scissors
- A ruler
- A compass and a pencil
- Red card, 15cm×15cm
- A hole punch
- Red thread

Christmas is celebrated around the world on 24th and 25th December. Presents are exchanged and, in some countries, cards are sent. Have a go at making your own Christmas card to send to your family and friends!

1 Stick some double-sided tape to a piece of gold card. Peel off the paper and stick on different-coloured ribbons.

2 Turn the card over and draw a 7cm circle using the compass. Cut out the circle to make an ornament.

Fold the red card in half and use the ornament as a template to draw a slightly bigger circle. Cut this out, leaving the rest of the card intact.

Use the hole punch to make a hole in the ornament. Hang it inside the hole in the red card using the red thread. Stick it in place with tape.

Decorate the card with presents made from squares of gold card and small ribbons.

The tradition of sending Christmas cards began in the UK in 1843.

Hanukkah card

This Jewish festival takes place in November or December, and lasts for eight days. Candles are lit on a special menorah, or candlestick, called a hanukkiah to celebrate, and children often receive gifts on each of the days.

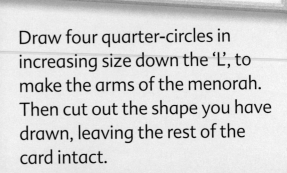

1

Fold a piece of the card in half, and draw an 'L' shape, 14cm long, 10cm wide and 0.5cm thick, against the fold.

2

Draw four quarter-circles in increasing size down the 'L', to make the arms of the menorah. Then cut out the shape you have drawn, leaving the rest of the card intact.

3

Tear off a piece of foil big enough to cover the card, and scrunch it into a loose ball.

4

Open up the ball of foil and tape it to the back of the card, then stick another piece of A4 card over it.

5

Make nine flames out of yellow and orange paper and stick them in place with sticky pads.

The Hebrew word 'Hanukkah' means 'dedication'.

Watch this step-by-step video of the Hanukkah card being made!

Diwali card

People celebrate the Hindu autumn festival of Diwali by decorating their homes with lots of clay lamps called 'diyas', candles and lights. Families and friends share food, exchange gifts and watch fireworks.

1 Fold the card in half. Cut two 7cm-long slits at the bottom of the card and a 2cm-long slit at the top.

2 Open this out and fold the card inside to make two sections pop out. Cut a piece of brown paper that is curved at both ends, big enough to cover the longer pop-out section.

3

Stick the brown paper to the long pop-out section and decorate it with lots of stickers.

4

Cut out a rectangle of red paper, and tape it in place onto the smaller pop-out section.

5

Make a flame from yellow and orange paper, and glue it to the candle.

The festival of Diwali is celebrated over five days, with the actual day of Diwali (the Hindu New Year) traditionally falling on the third day.

Holi card

You will need:
- Scrap card
- A pencil
- Scissors
- White card
- Scrap paper
- Coloured chalk
- Hairspray
- A4 piece of orange card
- Sticky pads

Holi is a Hindu festival to mark the beginning of spring. It is also known as the festival of colours or the festival of love. People celebrate by throwing coloured powders and dyed water over each other as well as eating and drinking with loved ones.

Draw a small hand shape onto some scrap card and cut it out to make a template.

Use the template to draw four hand shapes onto the white card. Cut them out.

3

Place the card hands onto the scrap paper, and use the chalks to colour them in.

4

Spray a thin layer of hairspray over the chalk to stop it from smudging.

5

Fold the orange card in half, and stick the hands to the front using the sticky pads.

People start celebrating Holi the evening before with a huge bonfire and lots of singing and dancing!

Glossary

confetti tiny pieces of coloured paper

dedication to be dedicated – devoted to something or someone

fasting going without food

forbidden banned from doing something

imprisoned put into prison

mosaic a picture made by fitting together small pieces of tiles or paper

silhouette a dark shape or shadow

traditional a way of doing something that has been passed on from generation to generation

Index